序

京沪高速铁路是集中展示我国经济实力、科技水平和综合国力的重大工程，是新中国成立以来一次性投资规模最大、技术含量最高的世纪性、历史性宏伟交通工程。

京沪高速铁路正线1318公里，其中桥梁244座，1059.7公里，占全长的80.4%；隧道21座，15.8公里，占全长的1.2%；路基242.5公里，占全长的18.4%。全线59次跨越既有铁路，41次跨越高速公路，99处跨越等级公路和城市主干道。多次跨越海河、黄河、淮河、长江四大水系的众多河流，其中Ⅴ级航道以上16处，全线特殊结构桥梁达397处。车站24座。设计时速350公里，初期运营时速300公里。

在党中央、国务院的正确领导下，在地方各级党委、政府的大力支持下，在铁道部的组织下，京沪高速铁路经过全体建设者三年半的奋战，于2011年6月30日通车。至今已安全运营了三年多，广大铁路员工按照"以人为本，精心服务"的理念，截止2014年9月，全线已安全运送旅客2.5亿人次，取得了良好的社会效益和经济效益。

《京沪高速铁路》画册以精美的图片真实记录了京沪高速铁路的勘测、设计、建设过程中建设者们顽强拼搏、开拓创新、无私奉献的精神风采。科学技术的创新，婀娜多姿的桥梁，穿山越岭的隧道，精雕细刻的轨道，功能齐全的车站，矫若游龙的动车组，安全可靠的指挥系统，颇具特色的服务品牌……为历史留下诸多珍贵镜头，也是献给国庆65周年的一份礼物。

京沪高速铁路股份有限公司董事长

2014年10月

PREFACE

The Beijing-Shanghai High Speed Railway is a historically magnificent transit engineering of the century, which attracts the largest investment and uses the most advanced technologies ever since the foundation of the People's Republic of China, and gives a full picture of the Chinese economic power, technical level, and the national competitiveness, etc.

The 1,318km trunk line of Beijing-Shanghai High Speed Railway includes 244 bridges with a total length of 1,059.7km, accounting for 80.4% of the entire length, 21 tunnels with a total length of 15.8km, accounting for 1.2%, and 242.5km subgrade, accounting for 18.4%. The entire line crosses over the existing lines at 59 locations, highways at 41 locations as well as the highways that are included in the road classification scheme of China and urban arterial roads at 99 locations. The railway, which has 397 bridges with special structure, also crosses over multiple waterways of the Hai River, Yellow River, Huai River, and the Yangtze River, including 16 spots of Grade-V waterways. There are 24 stations on the railway. The design speed for the railway is 350km, and the running speed of train on the railway at the initial stage of operation is 300km.

The Beijing-Shanghai High Speed Railway was open to traffic on June 30, 2011 after the hard work of three years and a half by all the working staff, which is under the effective leadership of Central Party Committee and the State Council with strong support from the local Party Committees and local governments on various levels, and organized by the MOR. The railway has been safely operated by the railway staff bearing the words of "providing human-oriented and quality service" in mind for over three years, and has safely originated 250 million passengers, bringing substantial social and economic benefits.

The album tells the true story of the Beijing-Shanghai High Speed Railway which includes the survey, design, and construction of this railway and its builders who work hard and dedicated themselves to this project and come up with creative solutions. The album is a gift for the 65th National Day, which shows many precious historical images concerning the scientific and technical innovation, all types of bridges, tunnels through mountains, fine rails, multi-function stations, speedy EMUs, reliable traffic control system, and service brand with unique features, etc.

.

Wu Qiang

President of Beijing-Shanghai High Speed Railway Corp.

October, 2014

目 录 》》
CONTENTS

宏伟 工程 >>> 008-137
Magnificent Project

京沪高速铁路从孕育到开工，经历了十余年的磨练，铁道部组织铁道第三勘察设计院集团有限公司、中铁第四勘察设计院集团有限公司、中铁大桥勘测设计院、中铁电气化勘测设计院、北京全路通信信号研究设计院的设计队伍，经现场勘测设计、多方案比选，制订了科学的建设方案，为中国铁路留下了宝贵的物质财富！

2008年1月16日，国务院批准京沪高速铁路开工，4月18日，温家宝总理宣布"京沪高速铁路全线开工！"十余万精兵强将，历经春夏秋冬的洗礼，饱尝严寒酷暑的考验，夜以继日，顽强拼搏，开拓创新，无私奉献，创造了一个又一个史无前例的奇迹，谱写了一曲又一曲气壮山河的凯歌！

A scientific building scheme for the Beijing-Shanghai High Speed Railway which is a great material wealth for China in railway sector and for which it took over a decade from its planning to the commencement of building work, was drawn up after field survey and design as well as comparisons among different proposals conducted by the design team organized by MOR with its members coming from the Third Railway Survey and Design Institute Group Corporation, China Railway Siyuan Survey and Design Group Co., Ltd., China Zhongtie Major Bridge Reconnaissance & Design Institute Co., Ltd., China Railway Electrification Survey Design & Research Institute Co., Ltd., and Beijing National Railway Research & Design Institute of Signal & Communication Co., Ltd.

The commencement of building work for Beijing-Shanghai High Speed Railway was approved by the State Council on January 16, 2008, and pronounced by the former premier Wen Jiabao on April 18 of the same year. More than 100,000 hard workers take a sustained effort to build the railway, developed creative solutions, and show intense devotion to work over the next few years, accomplishing an outstanding achievement.

和谐号动车组飞驰在京沪高铁线路上
A CRH Train at full gallop on the Beijing-Shanghai High Speed Railway

勘测设计
Survey and Design

1. 雪中勘测
   Survey on snowfield

2. 现场选线踏勘
   Field investigation for railway location

3. 铁三院设计人员群策群力优化京沪高铁设计方案
   Designers of the Third Railway Survey and Design Institute Group Corporation discussing optimal solutions for the Beijing-Shanghai High Speed Railway

天当被，地当床，冬天一身泥，夏天一身汗。京沪高速铁路的勘测设计人员跋山涉水，战天斗地，忠于职守，用智慧和汗水描绘着京沪高铁的绚丽蓝图。

The devoted survey and design team sleep outdoors through the entire year and conduct every necessary survey in order to get the precise data for design.

春

夏

1. 春风拂面时
   Field survey in Spring

2. 炎炎夏日中
   Field survey in Summer

3. 秋高气爽际
   Field survey in Autumn

4. 寒冬冰雪里
   Field survey in Winter

1. 水上勘测
   Field survey on the water

2. 中铁大桥勘测设计院进行南京大胜关长江大桥钻探
   Drilling by China Zhongtie Major Bridge Reconnaissance & Design Institute Co., Ltd. for the Nanjing Dashengguan Yangtze River Bridge

3. 山地钻探
   Exploration drilling in mountainous area

1. 水上钻探
Exploration drilling in river

2. 平原钻探
Exploration drilling on plain

3. 岩样分析
Rock sample analysis

1. 铁四院科技人员研讨优化设计方案
   Scientific and technical personnel from China Railway Siyuan Survey and Design Group Co., Ltd. discussing to optimize the design plan

2. 中铁大桥勘测设计院组织研究大胜关长江大桥设计方案
   China Zhongtie Major Bridge Reconnaissance & Design Institute Co., Ltd. holding a seminar on the design plan of Dashengguan Yangtze River Bridge

3. 中国工程院院士方秦汉、陈新、全国工程设计大师杨进参加南京大胜关长江大桥的设计方案研究
   Fang Qinhan and Chen Xin, the academicians from the Chinese Academy of Engineering, and Yang Jin, the engineering design master attending the meeting on the design plan of Dashengguan Yangtze River Bridge

4、5. 精心设计
   Meticulous design

桥梁
Bridge

>>> >>>

京沪高速铁路跨越海河、黄河、淮河、长江四大水系，正线上的桥梁共有244座、1059.7公里，占全线长的80.4%。其中，箱梁31013孔，各种特殊结构397处。

京沪高速铁路上的桥梁，犹如长龙，宛若彩虹，千姿百态。新结构、新材料、新工艺琳琅满目，桥梁的创新成果在这里被演绎得出神入化。

Beijing-Shanghai High Speed Railway crosses over the Hai River, Yellow River, Huai River and the Yangtze River, with 244 bridges totaling 1,059.7km long and accounting for 80.4% of the whole trunk line, among which there are 31,013 spans of box beam and 397 structures with specialized design.

These bridges, like flying dragons or rainbows, reflect different aesthetic concepts. Various new structures, materials and techniques are showcased for the bridges of Beijing-Shanghai High Speed Railway with big personalities.

和谐京沪高铁
When day

Beijing-Shanghai High Speed Railway

1. 开工前的施工测量
   Survey before construction commencement

2. 钻孔桩施工
   Construction of bored piles

3. "高空作业，安全第一"
   Safety first in high space operation

4. 桥墩钢筋绑扎
   Binding of steel bars for piers

施工中的桥墩
Bridge priers under construction

1. 制梁场
   Beam precast yard

2. 预制箱梁钢筋绑扎（长 32 米、重 900 吨箱型梁相
   当一个标准篮球场大）
   Steel bar binding for precast box beam（The size of a
   32m box beam with a weight of 900 tons is equivalent
   to the standard size of a basketball court.）

箱梁顶板钢筋入模
Construction of steel reinforcement for box beam

1. 箱梁混凝土灌注
   Concrete spouting of box beam

2. 制梁场夜战施工
   Construction by beam precast yard at night

3. 制梁场产品鉴定
   Product assessment of beam precast yard

4. 预制好的 900 吨重的梁
   Precast beam with 900 tonnes weight

900 吨提梁机和运梁车
A 900-tonne beam lifting equipment and transport trailer

1. 运输架桥机
   Bridge beam transport and erection machine

2. 京沪高速铁路架梁启动仪式
   Launching ceremony of beam erection for Beijing-Shanghai High Speed Railway

3. 跨既有京沪线架梁
   Erection of beam crossing over the existing Beijing-Shanghai railway

京沪高速铁路
桥梁正式架设仪式

深入学习实践科学发展观

中国铁建十四局集团

架梁
Beam erection

1. 架梁
Beam erection

2. 翘盼京沪高铁早开通
Eagerly looking forward to the opening of Beijing-Shanghai High Speed Railway

3. 特殊结构桥梁施工
Construction of bridge with specialized design

4. 建设者的喜悦
Joyful construction workers

1. 参加京沪高铁建设光荣
   Honored to be a construction worker of Beijing-Shanghai High Speed Railway

2. 淮河特大桥移动模架施工
   Construction by using the movable scaffolding and formwork for Huai River Super Long Bridge

京沪高速铁路跨京开高速公路 108 米钢箱拱桥
108m arch bridge of steel box on Beijing-Shanghai High Speed Railway crossing over Beijing-Kaifeng Highway

京沪高速铁路跨西黄左线及京山线空间钢架桥
Steel bridge of Beijing-Shanghai High Speed Railway crossing over Beijing-Huangcun railway and Beijing-Shanhaiguan railway

津沪联络线斜拉桥
Cable-stayed bridge of Beijing-Shanghai connecting line

沧德特大桥跨津浦铁路连续梁
Continuous beam of Cangde Super Long Bridge crossing over Tianjin-Pukou railway

独流碱河桥
Duliujianhe Bridge

济南黄河特大桥
Super Long Bridge of Yellow River, Jinan

跨济兖公路特大桥
Super long bridge crossing over
Jinan-Yanzhou Highway

荆河大桥
Jinghe Bridge

韩庄运河特大桥
Super Long Bridge over Hanzhuang Canal

京杭运河特大桥 86 孔连续框架桥（徐州东站北咽喉道岔区）
Continuous rigid-frame bridge with 86 spans over the Grand Canal (throat area to the north of Xuzhou East Station)

滁河特大桥
Super Long Bridge over Chu River

徐州东站桥群
Railway bridges at Xuzhou
East Station

浍河特大桥
Super Long Bridge over Hui River

淮河特大桥
Super Long Bridge over Huai River

南京大胜关长江大桥
Dashengguan Yangtze River Bridge in Nanjing

秦淮新河桥群
Railway bridges over the New Qinhuai River

1. 镇江京杭运河特大桥主跨
   Main span of the super long bridge over the Grand Canal in Zhenjiang

2. 龙虎塘立交 1-112 米提篮拱
   1-112m basket-handle arch of the Longhutang Grade Separated Bridge

3. 蕴藻浜特大桥
   Super Long Bridge over Yunzaobang River

丹昆特大桥（跨阳澄湖段）
Dankun Super Long Bridge over Yangchenghu Lake

上海"三角区"桥群
Bridges in Shanghai

隧道
Tunnel

>>>   >>>

京沪高速铁路正线上隧道共 21 座，总长为 15.8 公里，占全线的 1.2%。其中，最长的是济南—泰安区间的西渴马 1 号隧道，全长 2812 米。由于动车组在隧道中的运行速度很高（设计速度 350 公里 / 小时），带来空气动力学问题。因此，有许多技术难点需要在设计和施工中加以解决。

There are 21 tunnels on the trunk line of Beijing-Shanghai High Speed railway with a total length of 15.8km, accounting for 1.2% of the entire line, and the longest tunnel among them is the Xikema No.1 Tunnel in Jinan-Tai'an section with a total length of 2,812m. A lot of difficult technical issues concerning aerodynamics need to be resolved in design and construction due to the high speed operation of EMU train in tunnel.

欢悦
Great joy

掘进施工
Tunneling

技术人员在西渴马隧道研究设计施工方案
Technical staff having a discussion on the design and construction scheme outside the Xikema Tunnel

机械化出砟
Moving soil out mechanically

大型混凝土喷射机械手
Large-sized shotcrete robot

隧道仰拱移动栈桥施工
Building associated with tunnel invert conducted with movable trestle

1. 调度指挥中心对隧道施工进行远程实时监控
Real-time remote surveillance and control center for tunnel

2. 滕州隧道施工
Tunnel construction in Tengzhou

3. 隧道衬砌施工准备
Preparation for tunnel lining construction

建设者欢庆全线第一长隧西渴马1号隧道胜利贯通
Construction workers celebrating the breakthrough of No.1 Xikema Tunnel, the longest tunnel on the Beijing-Shanghai High Speed Railway

高速动车组穿行在西渴马 1 号、2 号隧道之间
A High Speed EMU running through No.1 Xikema Tunnel and No.2 Xikema Tunnel

竣工后的隧道
The tunnel completed

中铁四局施工的南京韩府山隧道群
Hanfu Mountain Tunnels in Nanjing, built by China
Tiesiju Civil Engineering Group Co., Ltd.

路基
Subgrade

>>> >>>

京沪高速铁路路基工程要求有足够的强度、刚度、稳定性和耐久性，必须满足铺设无砟轨道的要求。所以路基的工后沉降一般不应超过15毫米；路基与结构物间的工后差异沉降量不应大于5毫米。

The subgrade of the Beijing-Shanghai High Speed Railway must be of sufficient strength, rigidity, stability and durability to meet the requirements of ballastless track laying, therefore, the settlement after civil works shall not be more than 15mm, and the differential settlement at the transition sections between subgrade and structures shall be not more than 5mm.

地基加固——CFG 桩施工
Foundation reinforcement with CFG piles

1. 开挖
   Starting excavation

2. CFG 成桩
   CFG piles

3. 路基填筑
   Subgrade filling

4. 平整路面
   Leveling subgrade surface

1. 路基碾压
   Subgrade compaction

2. 路基检测
   Subgrade testing and inspection

3. 凤阳路基试验段
   Subgrade trial section in Fengyang

1. 美观的路基工程
   Artistic subgrade engineering

2. 路基边坡绿化
   Vegetation on side slope

3. 路基绿化
   Vegetation on subgrade

路基示范段
An exemplary subgrade section

轨道
Track

>>> >>>

为确保列车在高速运行下的安全性、平稳性和舒适度的要求，京沪高速铁路全线一次铺设跨区间无缝线路，除黄河、长江大桥外全部铺设无砟轨道。全线主要采用了 CRTS Ⅱ型板式无砟轨道。共铺设轨道板40多万块，由16个预制场生产。

The continuous welded rail is applied for the entire Beijing-Shanghai High Speed Railway, and the ballastless track, mainly CRTS II ballastless track, is used for the entire line except on the Yellow River Bridge and the Yangtze River Bridge. Over 400,000 slabs made in 16 precast plants are laid for the railway.

1. 安装轨道板钢筋网片
   Installing wire mesh for track slab

2. 轨道板混凝土布料
   Concrete paving

3. 打磨机自动控制
   Automatic control of grinding machine

4. CRTS Ⅱ型轨道板打磨
   Grinding of CRTS Ⅱ Slab

在轨道板上安装扣件
Fastener installed on the track slab

中铁十五局生产的成品轨道板
Slabs manufactured by China Railway 15th Bureau Group Co., Ltd.

轨道板铺设
Slab laying

1. CRTS Ⅱ型轨道板精调作业
   Accurate adjustment of CRTS Ⅱ slab

2. 轨道板精调
   Accurate adjustment of slab

3. 轨道板灌浆施工作业
   Grouting for slab

4. 枣庄至蚌埠先导段无砟轨道铺设标准化作业
   Ballastless track laying of Zaozhuang-BengBu pilot section

灌浆区

1. 双块式无砟轨道施工
   Construction of double-block ballastless track

2. 2010 年 7 月 19 日，京沪高速铁路铺轨仪式在徐州东站举行
   Track laying ceremony of Beijing-Shanghai High Speed Railway,
   Xuzhou East Station, July 19th, 2010

3. 徐州铺轨基地
   Track laying base, Xuzhou

4. 开始铺轨
   Commencement of track laying

京沪高速铁路铺轨施工
Track laying of Beijing-Shanghai High Speed Railway

1. 2010 年 9 月 29 日京沪高铁山东段完成铺轨
   Track laying on Shandong Section of Beijing-Shanghai High Speed Railway completed on Sep. 29th, 2010

2. 京沪高速铁路全长钢轨焊轨作业
   Welding of full-length rails of Beijing-Shanghai High Speed Railway

3. 道岔精调
   Accurate adjustment of turnouts

4. 铺设完成的高速道岔
   High speed turnouts

京沪高铁全线铺通现场
Track laying of the whole
Beijing-Shanghai High Speed
Railway completed

汤山路基轨道工程
Subgrade and track engineering in Tangshan

工程车在已铺设完毕的轨道上作业运行
Engineering car operating on the track after completion of rail laying

牵引供电
Traction and Power Supply

牵引供电系统是向动车组提供持续、充足、稳定的动力，保证动车组高速、安全、可靠运行的关键工程之一。

京沪高速铁路牵引供电系统主要包括三个子系统：一是变配电系统，包括沿线按一定距离分布的牵引变电所、AT 所、分区亭、开闭所等，其主要功能是将外部电力系统的 220 千伏等级的电源经调压后输送至接触网系统；二是接触网系统，包括支持装置、腕臂、接触网导线、承力索、分相装置等，其主要功能是将接触网导线上的 27.5 千伏单相交流电经由受电弓传送至动车组；三是为实现牵引供电安全可靠运行的远程监控系统，其主要功能是对牵引供电设备、接触网设备的控制、监测和保护等。

The traction and power supply system is one of the key engineering that supplies EMU with continuous, sufficient and stable power to guarantee high speed, safe and reliable operation of EMUs.

The traction and power supply system of Beijing-Shanghai High Speed Railway comprises of three subsystems: power transformation and distribution system, OCS system and protection and control system. The power substation and distribution system includes traction substation, AT post, sectioning post, switching post, etc., which are distributed along the line at certain intervals; it is used to transmit the regulated 220kV power from the outside electric power system to the OCS system. The OCS system includes support structure, cantilever, catenary, messenger wire and neutral section, etc. and is used to transmit the 27.5kV single-phase AC power from the centenary to the EMU through pantograph. The remote monitoring system is used to guarantee safe and reliable operation of traction and power supply and to realize control, monitoring and protection for traction and power supply equipment and OCS facilities.

1. 立杆作业
   Mast erection

2. 现场吊装硬横梁柱
   Lifting the headspan structure on site

3. 工厂预配接触网腕臂
   Prefabrication of cantilever in factory

4. 架设接触网导线
   Installing contact wires

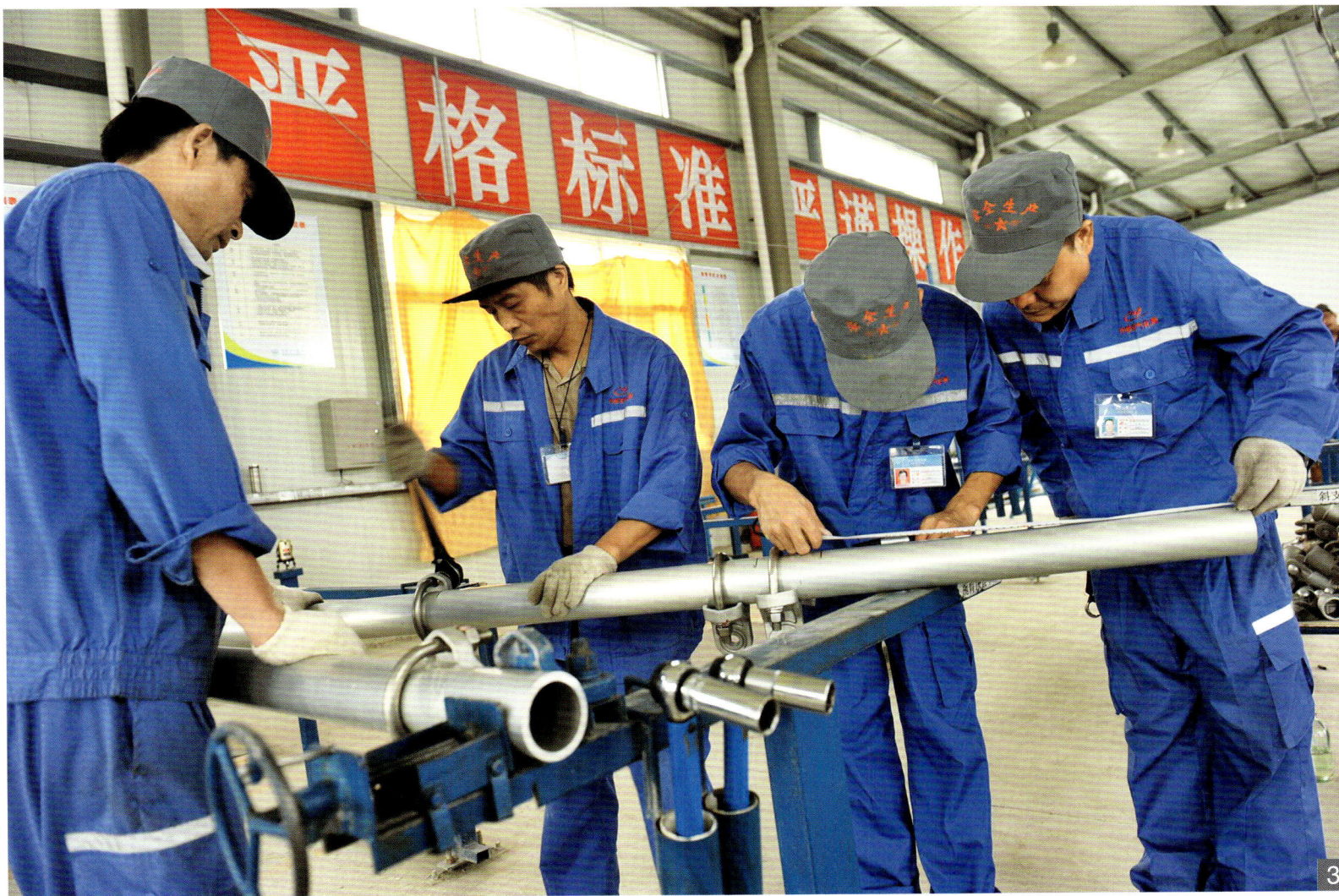

1. 架线车作业控制室
   Control cabin of OCS installation car

2. 恒张力架线车架设高强高导接触线
   Constant-tension OCS installation car installing high-strength and high-conductivity contact wires

3. 南京大胜关长江大桥架设接触网导线
   Installing contact wires on Nanjing Dashengguan Yangtze River Bridge

4. 电气化接触网高空作业
   OCS operation

勇攀高峰 追求一流

接触网架设起锚作业
Starting up the anchor section

1. 架线作业
   Wire installation

2. 接触网导线落锚作业
   Ending the anchor section

3. 工程技术人员用光学仪
   器定位接触网配件安装
   Technicians positioning the
   installation of OCS parts
   with optical instrument

顶风冒雪鏖战京沪
Working against wind and snow

1. 电力调度指挥中心对现场线路设备进行监控调试检测
   Electric power dispatching and commanding center monitoring and debugging field equipment

2. 变电站送电前的最后检测
   The last test of transformer substation before transmitting power

3. 南京南变电所全景
   Full view of Nanjing power substation

通信信号
Communication and Signaling

>>> >>>

京沪高速铁路通信系统具备可靠性、可用性、可维护性、可扩展性及安全性的要求。

通信系统为运输生产和经营管理提供稳定、可靠、畅通的通信手段，为列车控制、综合调度、旅客服务、电力及牵引供电等业务提供高质量的语音、数据及图像等综合数据传输。

通信系统主要包括：同步传输、数据网、专用移动通信、调度通信、应急通信、会议电视、时钟同步、视频监控、综合网管等子系统。

信号系统主要包括：行车调度指挥、列车运行控制、车站联锁与区间闭塞、集中监测等子系统。

The communication system of Beijing-Shanghai High Speed Railway meets the requirements of reliability, availability, maintainability, redundancy and safety.

The communication system provides stable, reliable and effective communication means for the transportation production and operation management; it also provides such integrated data transmission as high quality voice, data and image for the operation of train control, integrated dispatching, passenger service, electric power, traction and power supply.

The communication system mainly includes such subsystem as synchronous transmission, data network, dedicated mobile communication, dispatching communication, emergency communication, video conference, clock synchronization, video surveillance and integrated network management.

The signaling system includes such subsystem as train dispatching and command, train operation control, station interlocking and section block, and centralized monitoring.

安装完毕的道岔旁的联锁设备
Interlocking equipment installed beside turnouts

1. 产品组装
   Product assembly

2. 通信信号施工
   Engineering of communication and signaling systems

3. 安装分线盘
   Installation of distributing terminal board

4. 安装铁塔
   Installation of iron tower

1. 通信天馈线安装
   Installation of antenna and feeder for communication

2. 通信光缆敷设
   Communication cable laying

3. 站外信号设备安装
   Signal installation outside the station

4. 安装完毕的通信信号设备
   Communication and signaling equipment installed

1. 中继站箱式机房落成
   Box type equipment room for relay station completed

2. 仔细校核，确保零失误
   Carefully checking to ensure zero-failure

3. 无线通信基站
   Radio communication base station

3

现代 车站 >>> 138-163
Modern Stations

京沪高速铁路的车站融入了最新设计理念，体现了现代车站的功能，最大限度地保证旅客的乘车方便和安全，并充分考虑了与城市规划的协调，与地方交通的衔接。

　　全线 24 个车站如同镶嵌在京沪高铁黄金链上的一串宝石明珠，其风格各异，多姿多彩，汇历史于当今，融文化于土木，把京城历史、海派风格、儒家文化、园林艺术，尽纳入于当地车站建筑之中，展现出中华文明的深厚底蕴。

Based on the latest design concept, the stations along Beijing-Shanghai High Speed Railway embody the functions of modern stations. The convenience and safety of passengers are guaranteed and the coordination with the urban planning and the connection with local transports are given full consideration.

Total 24 stations on the railway are varied in style, just like a string of gems and pearls. The design of the buildings combines the local history and cultural characteristics by giving expressions to the history of Beijing, Shanghai style, Confucius culture and gardening art and shows profound implications of Chinese civilization.

北京南站
Beijing South Station

廊坊站
Langfang Station

天津南站
Tianjin South Station

天津西站
Tianjin West Station

沧州西站
Cangzhou West Station

德州东站
Dezhou East Station

济南西站
Jinan West Station

泰安站
Tai'an Station

曲阜东站
Qufu East Station

滕州东站
Tengzhou East Station

枣庄站
Zaozhuang Station

徐州东站
Xuzhou East Station

宿州东站
Suzhou East Station

蚌埠南站
Bengbu South Station

定远站
Dingyuan Station

滁州站
Chuzhou Station

南京南站
Nanjing South Station

镇江南站
Zhenjiang South Station

丹阳北站
Danyang North Station

常州北站
Changzhou North Station

无锡东站
Wuxi East Station

苏州北站
Suzhou North Station

昆山南站
Kunshan South Station

上海虹桥站
Shanghai Hongqiao Station

广大科技工作者和建设者依托京沪高速铁路这一实践平台，深入开展高速铁路基础理论和工程技术创新，取得了多项重要的科技创新成果。

以南京大胜关长江大桥为代表的深水大跨桥梁建造技术、CRTS Ⅱ 型板式无砟轨道成套技术、深厚软土松软土上路基沉降控制、最高运营速度 350 公里 / 小时的系列高速动车组、确保高速安全运行的 CTCS-3 级列控系统、节地绿化降噪环保技术等，都是我国高速铁路建设的成功实践。

By relying on the practices during the construction of Beijing-Shanghai High Speed Railway, a large number of technicians and builders have made innovations in basic theory and engineering technology of high speed railway and have made plenty of important achievements in technological innovation.

Successful practices of high speed railway construction are shown by deep-water and long-span bridges which is represented by Nanjing Dashengguan Yangtze River Bridge, a complete set of technical system for CRTS Ⅱ slab track, settlement control of deep soft soil and mollisol subgrade,350km/h EMUs, CTCS-3 train control system and technologies such as land saving, greening, noise control and environmental protection.

时速 400 公里的高速综合检测列车
400km/h high speed comprehensive inspection train

京沪高铁先导段高速综合试验

Integrated High Speed Test for Pilot Section on Beijing-Shanghai High Speed Railway

>>>   >>>

京沪高速铁路先导段综合试验历时 6 个月，累计试验里程 21 万余公里，试验共安装地面测点 2057 个，试验列车上安装测点 3615 个，完成了 9 大类 50 项综合试验。

在先导段先后开展了新一代高速动车组性能试验、高速综合检测列车检测系统试验、高速轮轨关系、高速弓网及供变电系统性能试验、路基和无砟轨道结构动力学性能试验、桥梁动力学性能试验、高速移动无线传输与列车运行控制试验、高速铁路空气动力学试验、环境效应试验等多学科范围、多专业领域的综合性科学研究试验。

京沪高速铁路先导段综合试验为深化高速铁路基础理论研究积累了数据，提升了我国高速铁路轮轨关系、弓网关系、空气动力学、电磁兼容、振动噪声控制等理论水平，总体技术达到世界先进水平，部分技术达到世界领先水平。

The integrated high speed test for the pilot section on Beijing-Shanghai High Speed Railway took 6 months and extended an accumulated test mileage of over 210,000km. By installing 2057 test points on the ground and 3615 test points onboard, 50 items of integrated tests involving 9 categories are completed.

Integrated scientific research and tests covering multiple disciplines and specialties were conducted successively on the pilot section, such as performance test for high speed EMU, inspection system test for high speed comprehensive inspection train, high speed wheel/rail interaction, performance test for high speed pantograph/OCS and power supply and transformation system, dynamics performance of subgrade and ballastless track structure, dynamics performance test for bridge, high speed mobile and wireless transmission and train operation control test, aerodynamics test for high speed railway and environmental effect test.

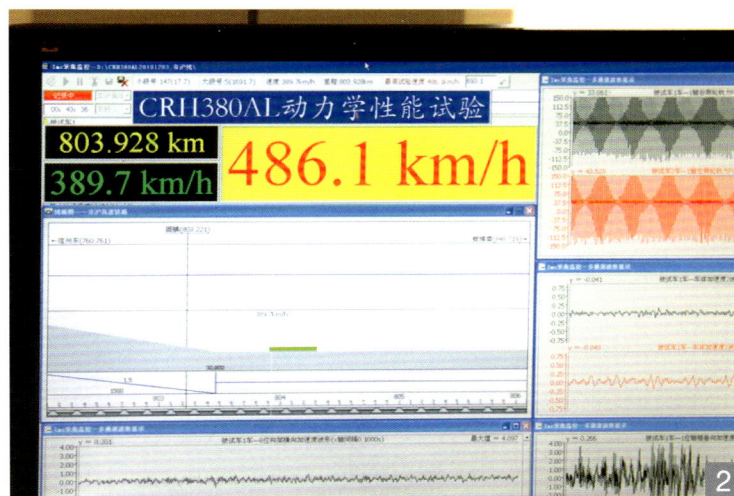

1. 综合试验中车厢的显示屏上显示出了 486 公里的时速
   The screen in the car displaying the speed of 486km/h during integrated testing and commissioning

2. 高速综合试验的电脑显示屏上显示出了 486.1 公里的时速
   The computer screen displaying the speed of 486.1km/h during integrated testing and commissioning

These tests have accumulated data to deepen the basic theoretical research for high speed railway and improved theory level in term of wheel/rail interaction, pantograph/OCS interaction, aerodynamics, EMC, and vibration noise control. The overall technologies have reached international advanced level and some have reached the world's leading level.

2010 年 12 月 3 日，国产和谐号 CHR380AL 新一代高速列车在京沪高速铁路先导段枣庄至蚌埠间综合试验中创下时速 486.1 公里的世界运营试验最高速度
The homemade "Hexie" CRH380AL, the new generation of high speed EMU, set the record of 486.1km/h for world's maximum speed of operation test on a pilot section from Zaozhuang to Bengbu on Beijing-Shanghai High Speed Railway on December, 3rd, 2010.

1. 京沪高速铁路首列轨检车通过淮河特大桥跨浍河系杆拱桥
   The first track inspection train for Beijing-Shanghai High Speed Railway running through Huai River Super Long Bridge over the Huihe River

2. 国产和谐号 CHR380A 新一代高速列车在试验中
   Homemade "Hexie" CRH380A, the new generation of high speed train in test

3、4、5. 铁科院科技人员在动车组上进行测试
   Technicians from China Academy of Railway Sciences conducting test onboard

1. 高速综合检测列车
   High speed comprehensive inspection train

2. 京沪高铁动车组试运行接触网检测
   OCS inspection for trial operation of EMU on Beijing-Shanghai
   High Speed Railway

3. 接触网短路试验
   Short circuit test for OCS

4. 接触网几何参数测试
   Geometry parameter test for OCS

5. 电磁辐射测试
   Electromagnetic radiation test

6. 车内噪声测试
   Interior noise test

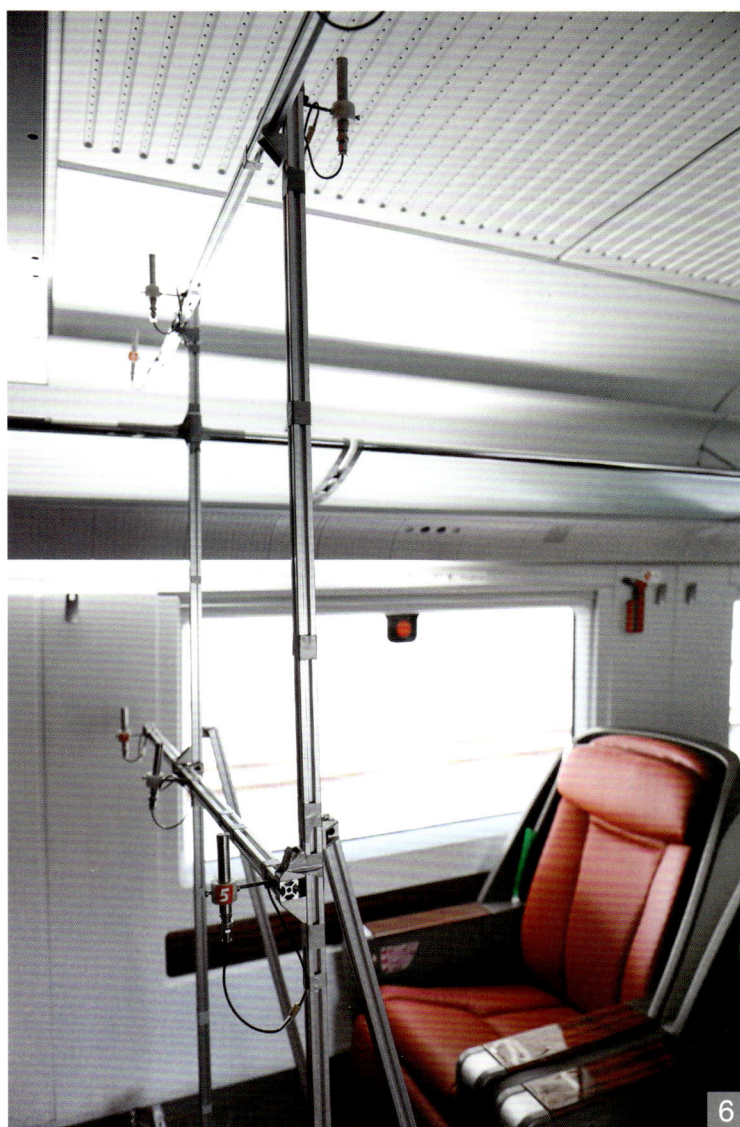

1. 检票闸机试验
Ticket gate test

2. 旅客引导信息系统测试
Test for passenger guidance information system

3. 声屏障隔声效果测试
Test for effect of sound barrier

4. 检测车通过淮河特大桥
Inspection train running through Huai River Super Long Bridge

5. 信号系统测试
Test for signaling system

6. 动车段下载试验数据
Downloading of test data at EMU depot

CRH380 新一代高速动车组
CRH380, New Generation of High Speed EMU

>>>　　>>>

　　京沪高速铁路上运行的 CRH380A、CRH380AL、CRH380BL、CRH380CL 四种型号的新一代高速动车组是由中国南车、北车集团研制生产。

　　CRH380 型新一代高速动车组在头车车形、转向架、牵引传动系统、制动系统、弓网技术、智能化、气密强度与气密性、减震、降噪、舒适性等方面实现了十大技术创新。从结构设计、运行控制、确保故障自动导向安全等方面，都做了多重保障。既能满足大众化乘车需求，也能给中、高端层次乘客提供优质的个性化服务，因此被中外媒体誉为"流动的星级酒店和商务中心"。

1. 待发的动车组
   EMUs ready for departure

2. 北京动车段全景
   Full view of Beijing EMU Depot

The new generation of high speed EMUs running on Beijing-Shanghai High Speed Railway can be classified into four types: CRH380A, CRH380AL, CRH380BL and CRH380CL, which are produced by CSR Corporation Limited and China CNR Corporation Limited.

Technical innovations have been made for CRH380 EMUs in ten aspects, to be specific, the shape of head car, bogie, traction drive system, braking system, pantograph/OCS interaction, smartness, airtight strength and air tightness, damping, noise control and riding comfort. Safety is guaranteed in multiple levels including structure design and operation control to meet the requirement of fault-safety principle. Besides meeting travel requirements of the public, they provide middle-level and high-level passengers with dedicated and high quality service and are called by domestic and foreign media as "the mobile starred hotel and business center".

1. 中国北车生产现场
   Workshop of China CNR Corporation Limited
2. 中国南车动车组制造车间
   EMU manufacturing workshop of CSR Corporation Limited

CRH380AL高速动车组　　　　　头车观光区

观光区
Sightseeing area

CRH380AL高速动车组　　　　　商务车

商务车
Business coach

CRH380A高速动车组　　　　　一等座包间

一等座车包间
Small compartment in first-class coach

CRH380BL高速动车组　　　　　二等座车

二等座车
Economy-class coach

新一代高速动车组 一等座车
First-class coach, new generation of high speed EMU

1. 新一代高速动车组乘务室
   Crew room, new generation of high speed EMU

2. 新一代高速动车组厨房操作台
   Kitchen, new generation of high speed EMU

3. 新一代高速动车组餐车服务台
   Service counter of dining car, new generation of high speed EMU

4. 在京沪高速铁路徐州东站整装待发的国产和谐号 CHR380A
   新一代高速列车
   Homemade "Hexie" CRH380A, the new generation of high speed
   EMU, well prepared for departure at Xuzhou East Station of
   Beijing-Shanghai High Speed Railway

5. 行驶在京沪高铁上的 CRH380AL
   CRH380AL running on Beijing-Shanghai High Speed Railway

北京动车段的"和谐号"
"Hexie" EMUs at Beijing EMU depot

黄昏下，CRH380BL 驶过南京秦淮新河桥群
CRH380BL passing by bridges of Nanjing New
Qinhuai River in the twilight

1. 一丝不苟
   Working in earnest

2. 北京动车所为动车组"体检"
   EMU inspection at Beijing EMU depot

3. 高速动车组奔驰在齐鲁大地上
   High speed EMU running through Shandong Province

以大胜关长江大桥为代表的深水大跨多线高速桥梁建造技术

Construction Technologies of Deep-water, Long-span and High-speed Bridges with Multiple Tracks, Represented by Dashengguan Yangtze River Bridge

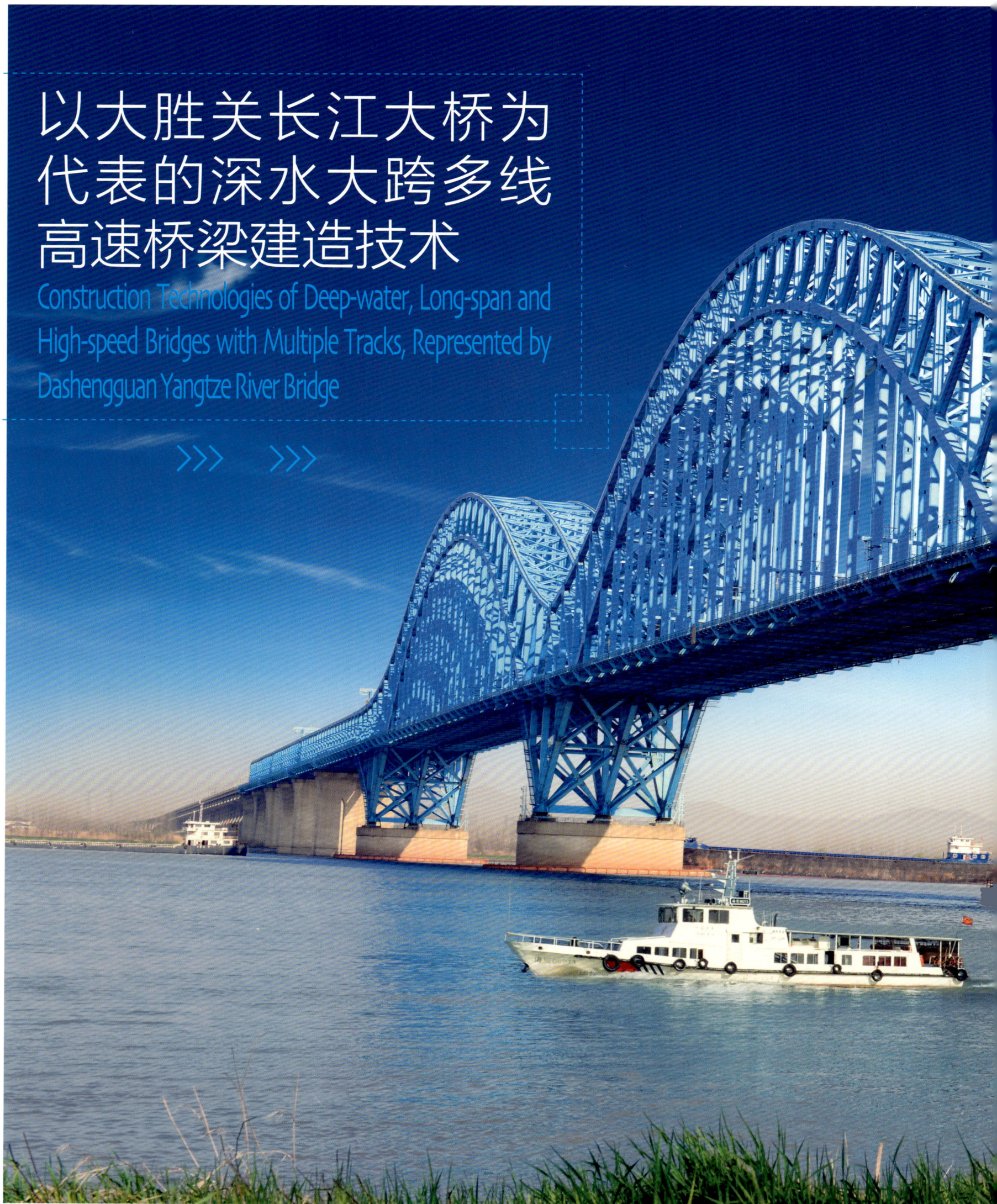

>>> >>>

南京大胜关长江大桥
Nanjing Dashengguan Yangtze River Bridge

南京大胜关长江大桥全长9.273公里（包括主桥和南北引桥），主跨为2×（84+84）米+（108+192+336+336+192+108）米钢桁拱连续梁，通航净高32米，能保证万吨级轮船顺利通过，是全线技术含量最高、跨度最长、施工难度最大的第一重点控制工程。它既是京沪高速铁路于南京跨越长江的通道，也是沪汉蓉铁路的越江通道，还是南京市地铁的过江通道。

南京大胜关长江大桥具有体量大、跨度大、荷载大、速度高的显著特点。

体量大　是世界上首座6线铁路大桥，钢材用量近8万吨，相当于武汉长江大桥的4倍，其中6、7、8号三个主墩，一个承台面积有7个篮球场大。

跨度大　主跨为336米，为世界同类级别跨度最大的高速铁路大桥。

荷载大　主桥恒载加活载约120吨/米；桥梁荷载35吨/米，相当于35个车道的公路桥荷载。支座最大反力达18 000吨，是目前世界上设计荷载最大的高速铁路大桥。

速度高　大桥上京沪线的设计速度为300公里/小时，为世界先进水平。沪汉蓉线的设计速度为250公里/小时，地铁的设计速度为100公里/小时。三条双线铁路共一桥的在世界上尚无先例，京沪高铁为首创。

该桥被国际桥梁组织授予国际桥梁界最高奖项——乔治·理查德森大奖，并被誉为"无与伦比"的创举。

1. 主墩钢围堰制造
   Manufacture of steel cofferdam for main pier

2. 基础施工
   Foundation construction

3. 主墩墩身施工
   Construction of body of main pier

Nanjing Dashengguan Yangtze River Bridge extends 9.273km (including main bridge and north and south approach bridges). The main span is designed as continuous beam of steel truss arches (2×(84+84)m+(108+192+336+336+192+108)). The navigable clear height of the bridge is 32m, guaranteeing the access of 10,000-ton ships. As the key engineering of the whole project, the bridge has the longest span with construction combining the advanced technologies and facing the toughest problems. The bridge is the passage for Beijing-Shanghai High Speed Railway and Hu-Han-Rong Railway crossing the Yangtze River, and also the crossing-river access of Nanjing subway.

Nanjing Dashengguan Yangtze River Bridge is featured by big size, long span, large loading capacity and high speed.

Big size: It is the first railway bridge with 6 tracks in the world, consuming nearly 80,000t steels which are 3 times heavier than that of Wuhan Yangtze River Bridge. There are three main piers, No. 6, No. 7 and No. 8; the area of the bearing platform equals to that of seven basketball courts.

Long span: With main span of 336m, it is the high speed railway bridge of its kind with the longest span in the world.

Large loading capacity: The dead load and live load of the main bridge are about 120t/m; the bridge load is 35t/m, which is equivalent to that of a highway bridge with 35 lanes. The maximum counter-force of bearings reaches 18,000t. It is the high speed railway bridge with the largest design load in the world.

High speed: Three double-track lines meet on the bridge. The designed speed of Beijing-Shanghai High Speed Railway is 300km/h, reaching the international advanced level, and the designed speeds of Hu-Han-Rong Railway and a subway line are respectively 250km/h and 100km/h.

The bridge is awarded with the George S. Richardson Medal, top award of the international bridge circle and is praised to be "incomparable".

1. 三片主桁新结构
   Three main trusses

2. 主墩墩身
   Main pier

3. 南岸眺望施工场景
   Construction scene overlooked from the south bank

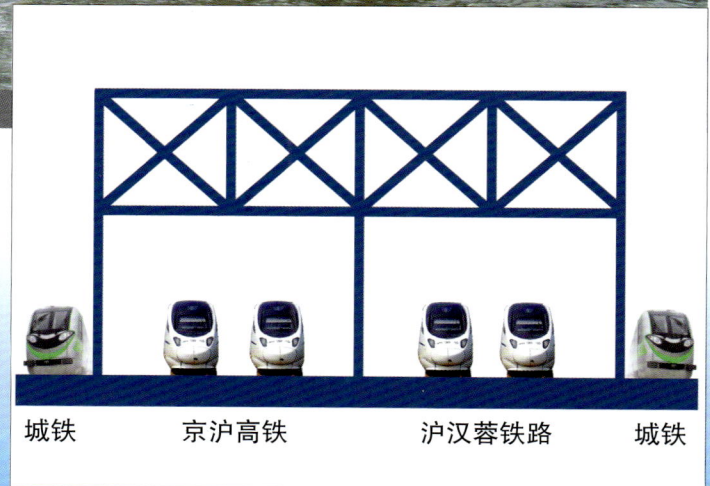

| 城铁 | 京沪高铁 | 沪汉蓉铁路 | 城铁 |

1. 起吊杆件
   Lifting steel members

2. 主墩钢梁架设现场
   Erection site of steel girder of main pier

3. 支座最大反力达 18000 吨
   The maximum reactive force of bearing
   up to 18,000t

4. 70 吨变坡爬行吊机在工作（俯视）
   70t gradient adjustable crawling
   cranes in operation（top view）

1、2. 建设中的南京大胜关长江大桥雄姿
Nanjing Dashengguan Yangtze River Bridge under construction

3. 斗酷暑
Fighting with the midsummer heat

南京大胜关长江大桥 70 米高吊索塔架
70m-high fastening stay tower of Nanjing Dashengguan Yangtze River Bridge

济南黄河特大桥
Jinan Yellow River Super Long Bridge

　　济南黄河特大桥全长 5 143.4 米，包括主桥、北引桥和南引桥。跨越黄河的主桥采用等高度刚性梁柔性拱结构。跨越南临黄大堤和北展大堤处采用 80 米预应力混凝土连续箱梁。主桥滩地采用 54.12 米跨度的预应力混凝土连续梁。其余南、北引桥采用 32 米简支预应力混凝土箱梁。

　　大桥主跨为（112+3×168+112）米刚性梁柔性拱四线铁路桥梁。两片主桁桁宽 30 米，目前在高速铁路同类桥型中居首位。

Jinan Yellow River Super Long Bridge including main bridge and south and north approach bridges extends 5143.4m. The main bridge crossing the Yellow River adopts flexible arch structure with equal-height rigid girders. 80m prestressed concrete continuous box girders are used to connect the north embankment and the south embankment; prestressed concrete continuous girders with span of 54.12m are used at the bottomland of the main bridge, and 32m simply-supported prestressed concrete box girders are used for south and north approach bridges.

The four-track railway bridge has the main span designed as flexible arch structure with rigid girders. The width of two main trusses reaches 30m, ranking the first of its type of all high speed railway bridges.

1. 超大孔径（直径 2.5 米）钻孔桩施工使用的钢套筒
   Steel casing pipe used for construction of bored pile with diameter of 2.5m

2. 1 号墩首桩开钻
   The first pile of No. 1 pier starts drilling

3. 建设中的黄河大桥桥墩
   The pier of Yellow River Super Long Bridge under construction

热烈祝贺京沪高铁济南黄河大桥1号墩首桩开钻

1. 桥墩施工
   Construction of pier

2. 主汛期施工
   Construction during the flood season

3. 钢梁架设
   Erection of steel girder

4. 桥面施工
   Construction of bridge deck

淮河特大桥
Huai River Super Long Bridge

淮河特大桥全长 85526.61 米，主桥全长 1051.52 米。桥跨形式为：（32+48+32）米连续梁 +（4×32）米简支梁 +（48+5×80+48）米连续梁 +（6×32）米简支梁 +（32+48+32）米连续梁。

The Huai River Super Long Bridge has a total length of 85526.61m and the main body is 1051.52m. Its formation is: (32m+48m+32m) continuous beams+4×32m simply supported beams+(48m+5×80m+48m) continuous beams + 6×32m simply supported beams + (32m +48m+32m) continuous beams.

1. 建设中的淮河特大桥主桥
   Main body of Huai River Super Long Bridge under construction

2. 架梁
   Beam erection

3. 淮河特大桥主桥晚霞
   Sunset glow on the Huai River Super Long Bridge

4. 动车组飞驰在淮河特大桥主桥上
   EMU galloping on the Huai River Super Long Bridge

镇江京杭运河特大桥
Zhenjiang Beijing-Hangzhou Grand Canal Super Long Bridge

镇江京杭运河特大桥，双线，采用（90+180+90）米 预应力混凝土连续梁拱桥结构，桥梁主跨为180米。这是目前世界上铺设无砟轨道铁路桥梁中同类结构的最大跨度。

Zhenjiang Beijing-Hangzhou Grand Canal Super Long Bridge, a bridge of double track, applies a (90m+180m+90m) prestressed concrete arch structure supported by continuous beams. The main span is 180m, which is the largest among similar type of railway bridges of ballastless track.

1. 桥墩施工
   Construction of pier

2. 镇江京杭运河特大桥 180 米主跨施工
   The 180m main span of Zhenjiang Beijing-Hangzhou Grand Canal
   Super Long Bridge under construction

3. CRH380BL 通过镇江京杭运河特大桥
   A CRH 380BL train passing through the bridge

丹昆特大桥
Dankun Super Long Bridge

丹昆特大桥自丹阳至昆山，全长 164.85 公里，为世界第一长桥。丹昆特大桥沿线跨越水面宽度 20 米以上的河道 100 余条（其中通航河流 36 条）；跨越各类等级公（道）路 150 余条，并 2 次跨越既有沪宁铁路，全桥共有 130 余处特殊结构梁。

Dankun Super Long Bridge, which stretches from Danyang to Kunshan with a total length of 164.85km, is the longest bridge in the world. It crosses over more than 100 rivers with width of water surface exceeding 20m (including 36 ones open to traffic) as well as over 150 roads of various levels. It also crosses over the existing Shanghai-Nanjing railway. Beams of special structure are used at more than 130 locations on the bridge.

1. 阳澄湖桥段的环保施工
   The Yangchenghu section built in an environmental-friendly manner

2. 丹昆桥架梁
   Beam erection on the Dankun Bridge

3. "和谐号"动车组飞驰在京沪高铁丹昆特大桥阳澄湖桥段上
   "Hexie" EMU galloping in the Yangchenghu section of Dankun Bridge on the Beijing-Shanghai High Speed Railway

1. "三角区"连续梁桥群施工
   Erection of the continuous beam in the "triangle" area

2. 京沪高速铁路跨既有京沪铁路、黄封铁路"三角区"施工
   Construction work in the "triangle" area

上海"三角区"桥群
Bridges in Shanghai

这里是京沪高速铁路正线及引入上海站上、下行联络线，沪宁城际铁路及引入虹桥站上、下行联络线共8条，新建高速线与既有沪宁铁路、黄封联络线之间立体交叉跨越而形成的一个狭小"三角"地带。有高铁、城际、普速铁路、联络线、动车走行线交错通过，实为上海市郊区一道不可多见的风景。

A narrow "triangle" area is formed by the mainlines of Beijing-Shanghai High Speed Railway (and its connecting lines), Shanghai-Nanjing intercity railway (and its connecting lines) and the Huangfeng connecting lines. All kinds of railways like high speed railway, intercity railway, conventional railway, connecting railway and EMU running track crisscross the area, forming a view rarely seen in the suburb of Shanghai.

北京南、上海虹桥等客运综合交通枢纽建造技术

Construction Technologies for Integrated Passenger Hubs
Like Beijing South and Shanghai Hongqiao Stations

>>>   >>>

京沪高速铁路首先提出高速客站一体化换乘的设计理念，北京南站是集普通铁路、高速铁路、市郊铁路、城市轨道交通与公交、出租等市政交通设施于一体的大型综合交通枢纽站；上海虹桥站是集航空、铁路、磁悬浮、城市轨道及市政交通为一体的综合交通枢纽。

京沪高速客站，更加注重室内外环境的缔造，通透、延续、开敞的空间特性，提高旅客出行的舒适度。

在高架候车厅、进站厅、站台及地下空间的设计中，多采用自然通风采光的方式，通过室内温度、声、光环境的控制，提升车站室内空间品质，体现了以人为本的理念。高速铁路站台面基本与动车组车厢地面平齐，方便了乘客上下车。

在车站设施布局中，将各种交通方式空间整合，并置、重叠、复合，充分利用车站的空间，极大地缩短了换乘旅客走行距离，实现"零换乘"。

在京沪高速客站中，部分"桥建合一"的高架结构，较好地满足建筑使用空间的要求。

The Beijing-Shanghai High Speed Railway has followed a "seamless transfer" design concept for the passenger stations. The Beijing South Station is a large comprehensive passenger hub integrating conventional railway, high speed railway, suburb railway, urban rail transit and other public transport modes like bus and taxi; the Shanghai Hongqiao Station is also a large passenger hub integrating air, railway, maglev train, urban rail transit and other transport modes.

The passenger stations on Beijing-Shanghai High Speed Railway attach more emphasis on the improvement of both indoor and outdoor environment, applying transparent, continuous and open spatial design to improve the traveling experience of passengers.

Natural ventilation and lighting are most applied in the spatial design of the elevated waiting lounge, entrance concourse, platform and underground space. The quality of indoor space in the station is improved and the passenger-friendly design concept is fully embodied via control on the indoor temperature, acoustic and luminous environment. The platform surface is basically level to the EMU compartment floor, which greatly facilities the getting on and off of passengers.

For the layout of station facilities, space is fully utilized via integrated and overlapped arrangement, which has greatly shortened the walking distance of passengers and realized indeed the target of "easy transfer".

Elevated structures combining the overpass and station structure also well tackled the issue of limited space.

北京南站风雨棚与站台
Canopy and platform in Beijing South Station

北京南站剖面透视图
Drawing of Beijing South Station

北京南站高架候车厅
Elevated waiting lounge of Beijing South Station

出了地铁上高铁

"One step" from the subway to high speed railway

1. 南京南站夜景
   Night view of Nanjing South Station
2. 南京南站剖视图
   Profile of Nanjing South Station
3. 南京南站斗拱结构
   Bracket system of Nanjing South Station
4. 南京南站高架候车层进站扶梯
   Escalators in the elevated waiting lounge in Nanjing South Station

昆山南站——京沪高铁与沪宁城际共用站
Kunshan South Station connecting Beijing-Shanghai High
Speed Railway and Shanghai-Nanjing intercity railway

上海虹桥站建设场景
Construction of Shanghai Hongqiao Station

上海虹桥站
Shanghai Hongqiao Station

上海虹桥站剖面图
Plan view of Shanghai Hongqiao Station

上海虹桥站——四通八达的电梯
Shanghai Hongqiao Station escalators and elevators to all directions

以高速接触网和 CTCS-3 为代表的四电系统集成技术

Integration Technologies Highlighted with High Speed OCS and CTCS-3 System

>>> >>>

　　京沪高速铁路牵引变电所全部是由两回路独立可靠的 220kW 电源供电，确保供电安全。接触网采用技术性能达到国际领先水平的高强高导铜合金导线。为满足 350km/h 运营速度及相应试验速度的要求，采用了新的张力体系和弓网匹配技术。

　　京沪高速铁路采用的是 CTCS-3 世界先进列控系统。它相当于人的大脑，是保障高速列车安全运行，提高运输效率的核心装备。在驾驶室的显示屏上，司机能看到前方 32 公里内的路况信息。同时，列控系统能对列车运行速度进行监督与控制，自动调整列车速度和追踪间隔。

The traction substations along the Beijing-Shanghai High Speed Railway all apply two separate 220kW power supply systems, which are reliable enough to ensure safety. World leading copper alloy wire with high strength and high conductive performance is used for the OCS. Updated suspension system and pantograph/catenary interaction technology are applied to cope with the demands of a running speed up to 350km/h and corresponding testing speed.

CTCS-3 train control system is used for the Beijing-Shanghai High Speed Railway, which serves like the human brain and is a critical equipment to ensure safe operation of high speed trains and enhance transport efficiency. Via the display in the cab, the driver can see clearly the track conditions within 32km ahead. The CTCS-3 is also capable of monitoring and controlling the train speed and automatically adjusting the train speed and tracing interval.

京沪高速铁路蚌埠牵引变电所
Traction substation in Bengbu

1. 建设中的高速接触网
   High speed OCS under construction

2. 动车司机操作室
   EMU cab

3. 上海虹桥站行车室
   Operation control center in Shanghai Hongqiao Station

4. 高速列车电气化
   Electrified high speed railway

上海虹桥站外牵引供电系统
Traction power supply system in Shanghai Hongqiao Station

中国铁路总公司调度指挥中心
Traffic control center in China Railway Corporation

深厚松软土地基处理和沉降控制技术

Thick Soft Soil Subgrade Treatment and Settlement Control Technologies

>>>   >>>

京沪高速铁路全线软土、松软土分布范围广。工程采用了高标准的地基加固处理技术和严格的路基填筑技术，确保线路下部工程满足高速列车运行的平顺性要求。

Soft soil and loose soft soil are widely distributed along the Beijing-Shanghai High Speed Railway. State-of-the-art subgrate reinforcement and filling technologies are applied to ensure that the substructure could meet the requirements of high speed trains for regularity.

1. 打入桩
   Driven pile

2. CFG 桩
   CFG pile

1. 路基施工
Subgrade construction

2. 路基过渡段施工
Construction of the transition section

3. 现场检测
Field inspection

4. 路基沉降观测
Subgrade settlement measurement

CRTSII 型板式无砟轨道和纵连式无砟道岔建造技术

CRTSII Slab Track and Longitudinal Continuously Prefabricated Ballastless Turnout Technologies

>>>　>>>

京沪高铁全线约 40 万块无砟轨道板，均采用工厂化预制生产，采用数控磨床对轨道板进行精密打磨，保证轨道结构的高平顺性。

无砟轨道板铺设过程中，采用自主研发的施工精调软件进行精确定位，误差小于 0.5 毫米。

高速铁路道岔的几何线形及位移控制都需要达到毫米级控制标准，技术结构复杂，是实现列车转换线路的连接设备。

京沪高速铁路在桥上岔区采用纵连板式无砟轨道，通过建立"岔—板—板—梁—墩"一体化的计算模型，编制了桥上纵连底座板岔区无砟轨道计算软件，将道岔、道岔板、底座板、梁体和墩台视为一个系统，充分考虑了各种力学影响因素，对无缝道岔、无砟轨道、桥梁强度和刚度稳定性检算，形成了系统的桥上岔区纵连板式无砟轨道设计方法和铺设方案，保证了桥上铺设 **18** 号和 **42** 号大号码无缝道岔的技术要求。

There are approximately 40,0000 slabs along the Beijing-Shanghai High Speed Railway, which are all prefabricated in batches in the factory. Digital grinding machine is used to fulfill accurate grinding of the track slab to ensure high regularity of the track structure.

Independently developed software is used for accurate positioning during laying of the slab track structure with error controlled less than 0.5mm.

The high speed turnout, known for its complicated structure, is a critical equipment for trains to transit between different lines and shall have its geometric alignment and displacement controlled with an accuracy of mm.

For turnout section on the bridge, a computational model for the structure of "turnout-slab-slab-beam-pier" is established, which considers the turnout, slab, base plate, beam and pier as a system, comprehensively taking into account all potential influencing mechanical factors to make computation of the strength and rigidity of jointless turnout, ballastless track and bridge so that a systematic design and laying scheme are tailor-made for the longitudinal continuously prefabricated ballastless turnout on the bridge. The No.18 and No.42 large jointless turnouts are laid with all technical requirement complied.

京沪高铁固镇板场
Slab yard in Guzhen

1. 京沪高速铁路 CRTS Ⅱ 型轨道板铺设标准化作业
Standardized laying of CRTS Ⅱ track slab on Beijing-Shanghai High Speed Railway

2. 道岔铺设施工
Installation of turnout

3. 轨检小车在检查轨道质量
Inspection trolley used to inspect the track quality

4. 铺设完成的高速道岔
High speed turnout laid

环境保护
Environment Protection

》》》　》》》

京沪高速铁路在工程建设中十分重视保护生态环境和水土保持。线路尽量绕避自然保护区、风景名胜区、饮用水源保护区、国家重点文物保护单位等环境敏感区；通过城市或居民集中地区时，采用适宜的降噪减振措施，满足国家环保标准和要求。路基边坡采用绿色植物与工程相结合的防护措施。

Great emphasis is attached to the protection of ecological environment and water / soil conservation during construction of the Beijing-Shanghai High Speed Railway. environment sensitive areas like natural reserve, scenic spot, protected source of drinking water, important national cultural relics are bypassed as much as possible; appropriate noise control and vibration mitigation initiatives are taken when the railway extends through urban or residential communities to meet the requirement of national regulations and laws for environment protection. The subgrade slope is also reinforced by multiple measures like planting vegetation or engineering measures.

1. 绿色掩映京沪高速铁路
   A green Beijing-Shanghai High
   Speed Railway

2. 护坡绿化
   Vegetation of side slope

3. 和谐京沪高铁
   Beijing-Shanghai High Speed
   Railway

1

1. 阳澄湖桥墩台围堰施工
Construction of pier and cofferdam of Yangchenghu Bridge

2. 阳澄湖大桥环保施工
Environmental-friendly construction of Yangchenghu Bridge

1. 禹济特大桥
   Yuji Super Long Bridge

2. 声屏障
   Sound barrier

3. 天津唐官屯梁场土地复垦
   Reclamation in Tangguantun beam yard in Tianjin

4. 绿化
   Vegetation

优质服务 >>> 246-287
Quality Service

　　京沪高速铁路自 2011 年 6 月 30 日开通运营以来，广大客运服务员坚持"以人为本，精心服务"的宗旨，热诚迎送四海宾客，帮助重点旅客排忧解难。旅客自进入车站，从问讯、购票、候车、购物，到检票、上车、乘车、下车，始终享受着温馨的服务，感受方便的旅行。京沪高速铁路打造具有自己特色的服务品牌。

Since the Beijing-Shanghai High Speed Railway opened to traffic in June 30, 2011, the entire staff has been following a tenet of "considerate service with passenger first" to serve passengers worldwide and help those target passenger groups to solve their problems. The passengers could enjoy intimate service during the whole journey, from entrance into the station, to enquiry, buying ticket, waiting, shopping, to check-in, boarding and getting off the train. The Beijing-Shanghai High Speed Railway has built up its service brand with unique characteristics.

问讯

Enquiry

>>> >>>

1. 北京南站润秋服务台
   Runqiu service desk in Beijing South Station

2. 天津西站服务台
   Service desk in Tianjin West Station

3. 济南西站问讯处
   Information desk in Jinan West Station

4. 徐州东站，回答旅客咨询
   Answer to the enquiry of passengers

1. 南京南站"美善空间"一瞥
   Help desk in Nanjing South Station

2. 南京南站功能完善的客服中心
   Customer service center with complete
   functions in Nanjing South Station

3. 常州北站"伴旅 519"服务台
   Service center in Changzhou North
   Station

4. 上海虹桥站问讯服务
   Enquiry center in Shanghai Hongqiao
   Station

京沪高速铁路
Beijing-Shanghai High Speed Railway

导向
Guide

>>> >>>

1. 天津西站，引导旅客候车
Guide for passengers to waiting lounge in Tianjin West Station

2. 北京南站候车大厅显示屏
Display in waiting lounge in Beijing South Station

3. 蚌埠南站引导牌
Guide board in Bengbu south station

4. 旅客通道引导
Guide sign

252

1. 引导旅客候车
   Guide passengers to the waiting lounge

2. 镇江南站引导牌
   Information board in Zhenjiang South Station

3. 上海虹桥站到达层的路标
   Guide sign in the arrival hall of Shanghai Hongqiao Station

4. 上海虹桥站旅客换乘
   Transfer of passengers in Shanghai Hongqiao Station

5. 上海虹桥站交通换乘指示牌
   Transfer guide in Shanghai Hongqiao Station

购票
Ticket Purchase

>>> >>>

1. 北京南站自动售票机
   Ticket vending machine in Beijing South Station

2. 各种购票专机
   Ticket purchase interfaces

3. 北京南站自动取票机
   Automaticing machine in Beijing South Station

火车票自动售票机

1. 南京南站自动查询机
   Automatic inquiry machine in Nanjing South Station

2. 北京南站售票
   Ticket window in Beijing South Station

3. 残疾人购票专窗
   Wheelchair accessible ticket window

4. 改签专窗
   Window for ticket change

候车
Waiting

>>> >>>

1. 旅客愉快地候车
   Enjoyable waiting experience

2. 上海虹桥站候车厅
   Waiting lounge in Shanghai Hongqiao
   Station

3. 曲阜东站候车室
   Waiting Lounge in Qufu East Station

4. 曲阜东站母婴候车区
   Mother/infant waiting lounge in Qufu East
   Station

邹鲁圣地 斯文在兹
WELCOME TO ZOUCHENG CITY
邹城
济宁欢迎您
方便出行
邹城
邹鲁圣地 孔孟桑梓
孔子
3

幼吾幼以及人之幼
4

1. 亲如一家
   Like a family

2. 济南西站候车室
   Waiting lounge in Jinan West Station

3. 济南西站候车室
   Waiting lounge in Jinan West Station

4. 南京南站贵宾候车区一隅
   VIP waiting lounge in Nanjing South Station

服务
Service

>>> >>>

1. 上海虹桥站欢迎您
   Shanghai Hongqiao Station welcome you!

2. 北京南站"润秋组全家福"
   A portrait for "Runqiu" service group of Beijing South Station

3. 北京南站，"小红帽"为您服务
   "Red hood" at your service in Beijing South Station

1. 天津西站竭诚为旅客服务
   Warm-hearted service in Tianjin West Station

2. 济南西站"泉馨青年志愿服务站"
   "Quanxin" volunteer service station in Jinan West Station

3. 南京南站"雷锋服务站"
   "Lei Feng" service station in Nanjing South Station

4. 扶送百岁老人上车
   Assist the senior people to get onboard

1. 济南西站全力做好新老兵运输工作
   Well prepared for transport of new soldiers and veterans in Jinan West Station

2. 南京南站，帮助老年乘客上车
   Assist the senior people to get onboard in Nanjing South Station

3. 上海虹桥站新的"风火轮"
   Segway HT in Shanghai Hongqiao Station

4. 北京南站保持设施干净整洁
   Facilities kept clean in Beijing South Station

购物
Shopping

1. 北京南站地下 1 层商业区
   Commercial area in 1st floor underground in Beijing South Station

2. 上海虹桥站候车大厅商业服务时尚精品店
   Shops in Shanghai Hongqiao Station

3. 天津西站商业区
   Commercial area in Tianjin West Station

4. 济南西站内特产专卖店
   Specialty store in Jinan West Station

1. 南京南站地方特色餐饮
   Local special restaurants in Nanjing South Station

2. 南京南站候车大厅内的小书屋吸引很多旅客
   Bookstore in waiting lounge of Nanjing South Station attracts many passengers inside

3. 徐州东站商业区
   Commercial area in Xuzhou East Station

4. 无锡东站内的特产
   Local specialties in Wuxi East Station

检票
Check-in

>>> >>>

1. 检票
   Check-in

2. 天津西站服务人员向旅客讲解自动检票闸机的使用方法和出行的注意事项
   The staff of Tianjin West Station is explaining to the passengers how to use the ticket gate and tips for travelling

3. 天津西站组织重点旅客提前进行检票进站
   Special passengers organized for early check-in

4. 北京南站检票
   Check-in in Beijing South Station

1. 实名验票
   Real-name check-in

2. 二代身份证验票机
   Ticket checking gate for
   second-generation ID card

3. 残疾旅客优先检票上车
   The physically challenged people
   given priority for check-in

4. 祝您一路平安
   Wish you a pleasant and safe
   journey!

5. 滁州站：欢迎劳动模范坐高铁
   Chuzhou station: welcome the
   model workers to take the high
   speed train!

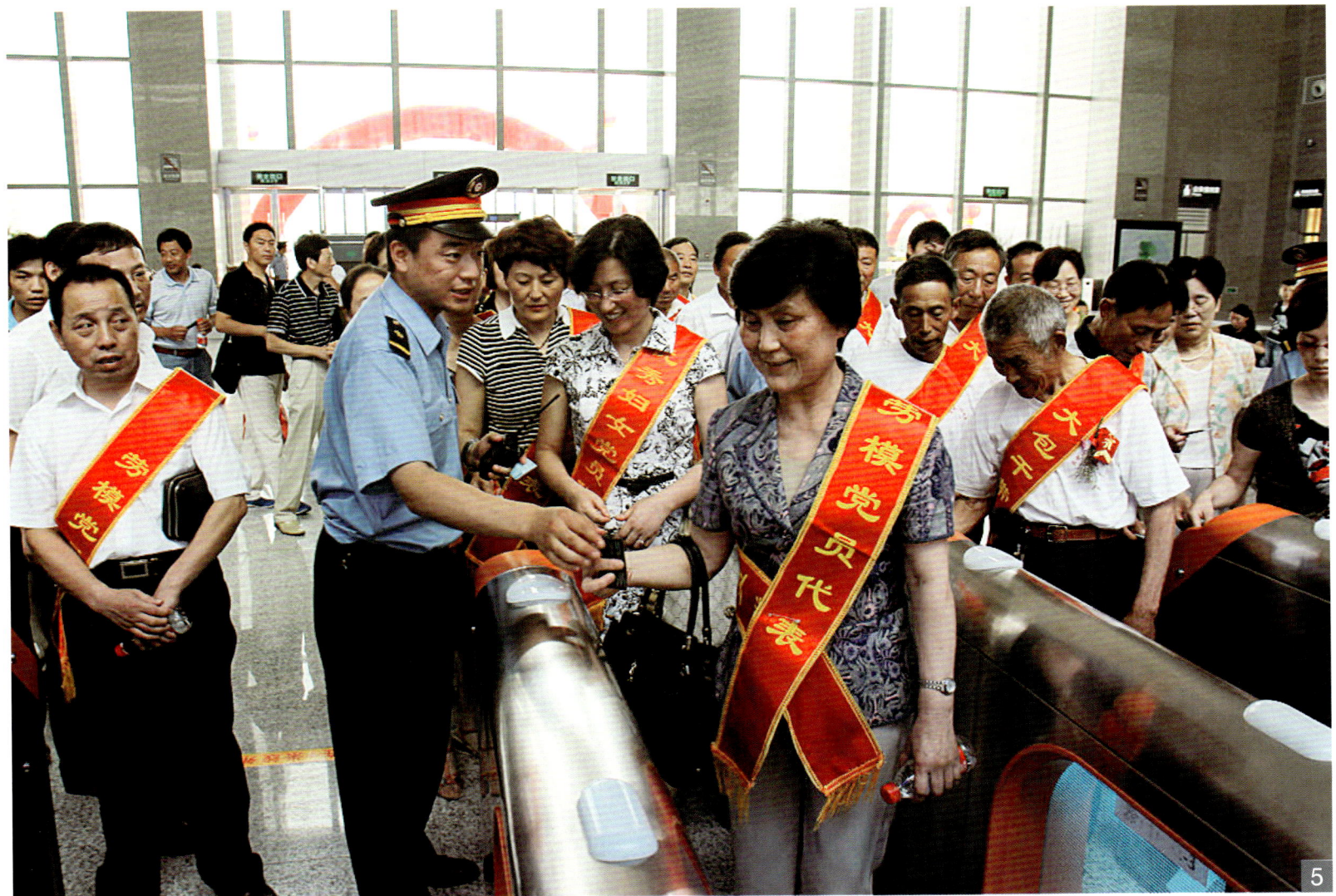

乘车
Boarding

>>> >>>

1. 列车工作人员主动引导旅客上车
   Guide the passengers to get onboard

2. 出乘
   Ready to set off

3. 欢迎四海宾客
   Welcome passengers worldwide!

4. 准备上车
   Ready for getting onboard

1. 上海虹桥站旅客有序登乘
Getting onboard in order in Shanghai Hongqiao Station

2. 重点照顾
Serving those with special needs

3. 有序上车
Boarding

4. 接发列车
Receiving the train

车上
On the Train

>>>　>>>

1. 为旅客供水
   Tea served onboard

2. "请您擦把手"
   Free warm towel

3. 爱心毯——服务重点旅客
   Blankets for those in need

4. "请看报"
   Free newspaper

5. 为了安全
   All for your safety

1. 京沪高铁车上开心的农民工
   Migrant workers enjoying their journey on high speed train

2. 重点照顾
   Special attention to those in need

3. 旅客在餐茶吧享受高铁服务
   Catering service in dining bar

4. 京沪高铁车厢平稳舒适
   Comfortable and stable compartment

5. "坐中国的京沪高铁，真爽"！
   Really cool! The Chinese bullet train!

6. 服务团体旅客
   Group passengers

7. 和谐之旅
   A harmonious journey

8. 快乐之旅
   A pleasant journey

9. 欢快之旅
   An enjoyable journey

下车
Arrival

>>> >>>

1. 到达
   Arrival
2. 无锡东站欢迎你
   Welcome you to Wuxi East Station!

3. 旅客出站
   Passengers exit from a station

4. 验票出站
   Check-out

5. 无锡东站地下停车场
   Underground parking lot in Wuxi East Station

6. 站外出租车
   Taxi outside

助推发展 >>> 288-311

An Impetus to Economic Development

京沪高速铁路的建成运营，有力推动了沿线经济的发展。地方政府把高铁车站作为城市新的地标，一座座高楼拔地而起，一家家企业汇集沿线，成为当地经济发展的新引擎。随着时间的推移，京沪高铁对沿线经济的拉动和辐射效应将释放出更大的潜能。

The construction and opening of Beijing-Shanghai High Speed Railway has dramatically boosted the economic development of regions along the line. The local governments take high speed railway stations as new landmarks of cities and many high-rise buildings spring up and numerous enterprises converge along the railway line, becoming an engine driving local economic development.

The Beijing-Shanghai High Speed Railway is sure to present more potential for its radiative effect and role in promoting the economical development of regions along the line.

上海虹桥站
Shanghai Hongqiao Station

廊坊车站周边繁华似锦
Boom around the Langfang Station

豪邸

1. 泰安站旁的新城
   New town near Tai'an Station

2. 枣庄高铁新城
   New town around high speed railway in Zaozhuang

3. 大企业落户德州东站
   Large enterprise headquartering in Dezhou East Station

4. 泰安规划的高铁新区
   New district under planning around high speed railway in Tai'an

济南西站周边崛起
Rise of the area around Jinan West Station

济南西站旁新建成的文化广场
Cultural plaza newly built near Jinan West Station

枣庄站周边建筑鳞次栉比
Rows of buildings around Zaozhuang Station

徐州东站周边高楼如雨后春笋
High buildings springing up like mushrooms around Xuzhou East Station

南京南站经济新区
Economic district in Nanjing South Station

常州北站周边的一座新城
A new town formed around Changzhou North Station

昆山南站周边的楼群
Complex around Kunshan South Station

春运期间，上海虹桥站繁忙场景
A busy scene during the Spring Festival peak season

SHANGHAI HONGQIAO RAILWAY STATION

上海虹桥新区
New town in Shanghai Hongqiao

后 记

　　京沪高速铁路，2008年1月国家批准开工建设，2011年6月30日建成投入运营，建设期历时3年半；到2014年10月，又已安全运营3年多。为反映京沪高速铁路建设的辉煌成就，展示广大科技工作者和十余万建设大军辛勤劳动的成果，并彰显客服人员的华丽风采和旅客出行"安全、快捷、方便 、舒适"的服务，京沪高速铁路股份有限公司决定组织编辑《京沪高速铁路》画册，也是献给中华人民共和国建国65周年的一份礼物。

　　为了使《画册》的内容相对系统，图片更加精美，编者除从原建设、运营单位提供的大量图片中优中选优外，京沪高速铁路股份有限公司崔喜利同志、中国铁道出版社王楠同志又多次去京沪高速铁路现场拍摄新的与时俱进的图片。在这里，特向提供图片的单位和摄影爱好者表示感谢！

　　《画册》初步设计完成后，编委会专门召开会议，对结构布局、图片选择、内容介绍、文字说明等进行了逐项讨论。京沪高速铁路股份有限公司原董事长蔡庆华对《画册》作了终审。

　　《画册》英文由中国铁道科学研究院科学技术信息研究所陈琦、陈敏、韩旭翻译；刘大磊、张昱辰、武亚玲核校。

　　中国铁道出版社编审丁国平负责《画册》的文字撰写、选图和编辑工作。

编 者

2014年10月

POSTSCRIPT

The Beijing-Shanghai High Speed Railway was formally approved for construction in January, 2008 and entered commercial service in June 30, 2011, of which the construction work lasted about 3 years and a half. Safe operation has been maintained for more than 3 years by October 2014. To demonstrate the brilliant achievements of the Beijing-Shanghai High Speed Railway and the hard work of those scientific workers and over 10,0000 construction workers, and in the meanwhile show the elegant bearing of the passenger service staff and their "safe, efficient, convenient and comfortable" service provided to the passengers, the "Picture Album of Beijing-Shanghai High Speed Railway" is compiled by the Beijing-Shanghai High Speed Railway Corporation, also as a gift to the 65 years anniversary of the founding of the People's Republic of China.

To make the album content-rich and exquisite, pictures are selected elaborately among those provided by the construction and operation units. Mr. Cui Xili from the Beijing-Shanghai High Speed Railway Corporation and Mr. Wang Nan from China Railway Publishing House went to the Beijing-Shanghai High Speed Railway site for many times to have taken many pictures keeping pace with times. We hereby acknowledge those organizations and photographers providing pictures for their contributions to this album.

After the preliminary design finished, the editorial board held many special meetings to have discussion on the layout, image and literal content of the album. Mr. Cai Qinghua, the former president of Beijing-Shanghai High Speed Railway Corporation, conducted final review of the album.

The English edition of the album is translated by Chen Qi, Chen Min and Han Xu, and checked by Liu Dalei, Zhang Yuchen and Wu Yaling from the Scientific and Technological Information Research Institute of China Academy of Railway Sciences.

Mr. Ding Guoping, senior editor from China Railway Publishing House, takes full charge of writing of the literal content, picture selection and the edit work of the album.

Editor

October, 2014

鸣　谢

　　本《画册》在编辑中，除使用京沪高速铁路股份有限公司的图片外，各设计、施工、运营管理单位的宣传部门提供了大量的资料图片，主要有：

　　铁道第三勘察设计院集团有限公司，中铁第四勘察设计院集团有限公司，中铁电气化勘测设计研究院有限公司，中国铁路通信信号集团公司，北京全路通信信号研究设计院，中铁大桥勘测设计院有限公司，中铁大桥工程局，中铁一局集团，中铁二局集团，中铁三局集团，中铁四局集团，中铁五局集团，中铁六局集团，中铁八局集团，中铁十局集团，中铁十一局集团，中铁十二局集团，中铁十四局集团，中铁十五局集团，中铁十六局集团，中铁十七局集团，中铁十八局集团，中铁十九局集团，中国交通建设集团，中国水利水电建设集团，上海铁路局上海铁路枢纽工程建设指挥部、上海铁路局南京南站工程建设指挥部，中国北车集团，中国南车集团，北京铁路局、济南铁路局、上海铁路局宣传部等。

　　铁道科学研究院也提供了大量图片。

　　在此一并致以诚挚的感谢！

　　图片摄影作者有：

丁万斌　崔喜利　王　楠　王劲松　李　敏　张志国　刘新红　陈　敬
杜振珂　刘国占　山　佳　顾　亚　冯学亮　张艳超　武　羽　贾国春
闫　东　刘小果　何俊昌　高　群　陈志一　杨晓鹏　杨卧龙　李立国
刘　鹏　李忠民　胡　山　黄山森　董海伟　王　冬　罗春晓　原瑞伦
郭　平　吴兴锋　杨　浩　杨　洋　吴宏道　赵志刚　曹　宁　高卫生
房秀龙　王　利　王秀歧　赵湘明　乔　力　严　勇　郭润滋　王济林
周兰新　夏　冉　索　威　张学忠　李文伟　张卫东　王玉建　朱　河
李　荫　陆祖韬　冯　博　杜建雄　李　皓　陈晓倩　戴淮林　杨　光
葛爱民　李　超　胡　健　戴　兵　朱怀宝　傅　兴　杨超英　王秋林
孔庆宽　刘明汉　奚　平　陶　航　何　鸣　王宝宝　陈　益　徐二中
沈首军　陆应果　杨光和　张　磊　张　巍　高红召

　　有的照片由于作者不详，未能署名，知情者或本人请及时来电来信，我们将在重印时补署作者名字。谨致敬意！

编　者
2014年10月

ACKNOWLEDGEMENT

In addition to the pictures provided by Beijing-Shanghai High Speed Railway Corporation, the album has also adopted a large quantity of pictures provided by the following organizations:

The 3rd Railway Survey & Design Institute Group Corporation, China Railway Siyuan Survey and Design Group Co, Ltd, China Railway Electrification Survey Design & Research Institute Co. Ltd, China Railway Signal & Communication Corp., Beijing National Railway Research & design Institute of Signal &Communication Co. Ltd, China Railway Major Bridge Reconnaissance & Design Institute Co., Ltd, China Railway Major Bridge Engineering Group Co.,Ltd, China Railway First Group Co., ltd, China Railway No.2 Engineering Group Co., Ltd, China Railway No.3 Engineering Group Co., Ltd, China Tiesiju Civil Engineering Group Co., Ltd, China Railway No.5 Engineering Group Co., Ltd, the 6th Engineering Bureau, CREC, China Railway No.8 Engineering Group Co., Ltd, China Railway 10th Engineering Group Co., Ltd, China Railway 11th Engineering Group Co., Ltd, China Railway 12th Bureau Group Co., Ltd, China Railway 14th Construction Bureau Co., Ltd, China Railway 15th Bureau Group Co., Ltd, China Railway 16th Bureau Group Co., Ltd, China Railway 17th Bureau Group Co., Ltd, China Railway 18th Bureau Group Co., Ltd, China Railway 19th Bureau Group Co., Ltd, China Communications Construction Company Ltd, Sinohydro Group, Project Headquarter for Shanghai Railway Terminal of Shanghai Railway Administration, Project Headquarter for Nanjing South Station of Shanghai Railway Administration, Equipment Department of the Transportation Bureau of the Ministry of Railways, CNR, CSR, Beijing Railway Administration, Jinan Railway Administration, the Publicity Department of Shanghai Railway Administration, etc.

China Academy of Railway Sciences also provides many pictures for the album.

We hereby acknowledge those organizations for their contributions to this album.

Photographers include:

Ding Wanbin, Cui Xili, Wang Nan, Wang Jinsong, Li Min, Zhang Zhiguo, Liu Xinhong, Chen Jing, Du Zhenke, Liu Guozhan, Shan Jia, Gu Ya, Feng Xueliang, Zhang Yanchao, Wu Yu, Jia Guochun, Yan Dong, Liu Xiaoguo, He Junchang, Gao Qun, Chen Zhiyi, Yang Xiaopeng, Yang Wolong, Li Liguo, Liu Peng, Li Zhongmin, Hu Shan, Huang Shansen, Dong Haiwei, Wang Dong, Luo Chunxiao, Yuan Ruilun, Guo Ping, Wu Xingfeng, Yang Hao, Yang Yang, Wu Hongdao, Zhao Zhigang, Cao Ning, Gao Weisheng, Fang Xiulong, Wang Li, Wang Xiuqi, Zhao Xiangming, Qiao Li, Yan Yong, Guo Runzi, Wang Jilin, Zhou Lanxin, Xia Ran, Suo Wei, Zhang Xuezhong, Li Wenwei, Zhang Weidong, Wang Yujian, Zhu He, Li Yinlu, Zu Tao, Feng Bo, Du Jianxiong, Li Hao, Chen Xiaoqian, Dai Huailin, Yang Guang, Ge Aimin, Li Chao, Hu Jian, Dai Bing, Zhu Huaibao, Fu Xing, Yang Chaoying, Wang Qiulin, Kong Qingkuan, Liu Minghan, Xi Ping, Tao Hang, He Wu, Wang Baobao, Chen Yi, Xu Erzhong, Shen Shoujun, Lu Yingguo, Yang Guanghe, Zhang Lei, Zhang Wei, Gao Hongzhao

Some pictures are not affixed since their photographers are not found. The photographers or anyone who knows their photographers please call us or write to us. We will add your names when the album is republished.

Editor

October, 2014